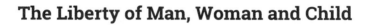

The Liberty of Man, Woman and Child

THE

Liberty of Man, Woman and Child.

A LECTURE

BY

ROBERT G. INGERSOLL.

ALSO

A TRIBUTE TO HIS BROTHER

EBON C. INGERSOLL.

Liberty sustains the same relation to mind that space does to matter.

NEW YORK
C. P. FARRELL, PUBLISHER
1915

THE LIBERTY OF

MAN, WOMAN AND CHILD.

LIBERTY SUSTAINS THE SAME RELATION TO MIND THAT SPACE DOES TO MATTER.

THERE is no slavery but ignorance.   Liberty is the child of intelligence.

The history of man is simply the history of slavery, of injustice and brutality, together with the means by which he has, through the dead and desolate years, slowly and painfully advanced.   He has been the sport and prey of priest and king, the food of superstition and cruel might.   Crowned force has governed ignorance through fear.   Hypocrisy and tyranny — two vultures — have fed upon the liberties of man.   From all these there has been, and is, but one means of escape — intellectual development.   Upon the back of industry has been the whip.   Upon the brain have been the fetters of superstition.   Nothing has been left

undone by the enemies of freedom. Every art
and artifice, every cruelty and outrage has been
practiced and perpetrated to destroy the rights of
man. In this great struggle every crime has been
rewarded and every virtue has been punished.
Reading, writing, thinking and investigating have
all been crimes.

Every science has been an outcast.

All the altars and all the thrones united to
arrest the forward march of the human race. The
king said that mankind must not work for themselves. The priest said that mankind must not
think for themselves. One forged chains for the
hands, the other for the soul. Under this infamous
regime the eagle of the human intellect was for
ages a slimy serpent of hypocrisy.

The human race was imprisoned. Through
some of the prison bars came a few struggling rays
of light. Against these bars Science pressed its
pale and thoughtful face, wooed by the holy dawn
of human advancement. Bar after bar was broken
away. A few grand men escaped and devoted
their lives to the liberation of their fellows.

Only a few years ago there was a great
awakening of the human mind. Men began to

inquire by what right a crowned robber made them work for him? The man who asked this question was called a traitor. Others asked by what right does a robed hypocrite rule my thought? Such men were called infidels. The priest said, and the king said, where is this spirit of investigation to stop? They said then and they say now, that it is dangerous for man to be free. I deny it. Out on the intellectual sea there is room enough for every sail. In the intellectual air there is space enough for every wing.

The man who does not do his own thinking is a slave, and is a traitor to himself and to his fellowmen.

Every man should stand under the blue and stars, under the infinite flag of nature, the peer of every other man.

Standing in the presence of the Unknown, all have the same right to think, and all are equally interested in the great questions of origin and destiny. All I claim, all I plead for, is liberty of thought and expression. That is all. I do not pretend to tell what is absolutely true, but what I think is true. I do not pretend to tell all the truth.

I do not claim that I have floated level with the

heights of thought, or that I have descended to the very depths of things. I simply claim that what ideas I have, I have a right to express; and that any man who denies that right to me is an intellectual thief and robber. That is all.

Take those chains from the human soul. Break those fetters. If I have no right to think, why have I a brain? If I have no such right, have three or four men, or any number, who may get together, and sign a creed, and build a house, and put a steeple upon it, and a bell in it—have they the right to think? The good men, the good women are tired of the whip and lash in the realm of thought. They remember the chain and fagot with a shudder. They are free, and they give liberty to others. Whoever claims any right that he is unwilling to accord to his fellow-men is dishonest and infamous.

In the good old times, our fathers had the idea that they could make people believe to suit them. Our ancestors, in the ages that are gone, really believed that by force you could convince a man. You cannot change the conclusion of the brain by torture; nor by social ostracism. But I will tell you what you can do by these, and what you have done. You can make hypocrites by the million. You can make a man say that he has changed his mind; but he remains of the same opinion still. Put fetters all over him; crush his feet in iron boots; stretch him to the last gasp upon the holy rack; burn him, if you please, but his ashes will be of the same opinion still.

Our fathers in the good old times—and the best thing I can say about them is, that they have passed away—had an idea that they could force men to think their way. That idea is still prevalent in many parts, even of this country. Even in our day some extremely religious people say, "We will not trade with that man; we will not vote for him; we will not hire him if he is a lawyer; we will die before we will take his medicine if he is a doctor; we will not invite him to dinner; we will socially ostracise him; he must come to our church; he must believe our doctrines; he must worship our god or we will not in any way contribute to his support."

In the old times of which I have spoken, they desired to make all men think exactly alike. All the mechanical ingenuity of the world cannot make two clocks run exactly alike, and how are you

going to make hundreds of millions of people, dif-
fering in brain and disposition, in education and
aspiration, in conditions and surroundings, each
clad in a living robe of passionate flesh — how are
you going to make them think and feel alike? If
there is an infinite god, one who made us, and
wishes us to think alike, why did he give a spoonful
of brains to one, and a magnificent intellectual
development to another? Why is it that we have
all degrees of intelligence, from orthodoxy to
genius, if it was intended that all should think and
feel alike?

I used to read in books how our fathers perse-
cuted mankind. But I never appreciated it. I read
it, but it did not burn itself into my soul. I did not
really appreciate the infamies that have been committed in the name of religion, until I saw the iron
arguments that Christians used. I saw the Thumb-
screw — two little pieces of iron, armed on the
inner surfaces with protuberances, to prevent their
slipping ; through each end a screw uniting the two
pieces. And when some man denied the efficacy
of baptism, or may be said, "I do not believe that
a fish ever swallowed a man to keep him from
drowning," then they put his thumb between these

pieces of iron and in the name of love and universal forgiveness, began to screw these pieces together. When this was done most men said, ''I will recant.'' Probably I should have done the same. Probably I would have said : '' Stop ; I will admit anything that you wish; I will admit that there is one god or a million, one hell or a billion; suit yourselves; but stop.''

But there was now and then a man who would not swerve the breadth of a hair. There was now and then some sublime heart, willing to die for an intellectual conviction. Had it not been for such men, we would be savages to-night. Had it not been for a few brave, heroic souls in every age, we would have been cannibals, with pictures of wild beasts tattooed upon our flesh, dancing around some dried snake fetich.

Let us thank every good and noble man who stood so grandly, so proudly, in spite of opposition, of hatred and death, for what he believed to be the truth.

Heroism did not excite the respect of our fathers. The man who would not recant was not forgiven. They screwed the thumbscrews down to the last pang, and then threw their victim into some

dungeon, where, in the throbbing silence and darkness, he might suffer the agonies of the fabled
damned. This was done in the name of love—in
the name of mercy—in the name of the compas-
sionate Christ.

I saw, too, what they called the Collar of
Torture. Imagine a circle of iron, and on the
inside a hundred points almost as sharp as needles.
This argument was fastened about the throat of
the sufferer. Then he could not walk, nor sit
down, nor stir without the neck being punctured by
these points. In a little while the throat would
begin to swell, and suffocation would end the
agonies of that man. This man, it may be, had
committed the crime of saying, with tears upon his
cheeks, "I do not believe that God, the father of
us all, will damn to eternal perdition any of the
children of men."

I saw another instrument, called the Scaven-
ger's Daughter. Think of a pair of shears with
handles, not only where they now are, but at the
points as well, and just above the pivot that unites
the blades, a circle of iron. In the upper handles
the hands would be placed; in the lower, the feet;
and through the iron ring, at the centre, the head

of the victim would be forced. In this condition, he would be thrown prone upon the earth, and the strain upon the muscles produced such agony that insanity would in pity end his pain.

This was done by gentlemen who said: "Whosoever smiteth thee upon one cheek turn to him the other also."

I saw the Rack. This was a box like the bed of a wagon, with a windlass at each end, with levers, and ratchets to prevent slipping; over each windlass went chains; some were fastened to the ankles of the sufferer; others to his wrists. And then priests, clergymen, divines, saints, began turning these windlasses, and kept turning, until the ankles, the knees, the hips, the shoulders, the elbows, the wrists of the victim were all dislocated, and the sufferer was wet with the sweat of agony. And they had standing by a physician to feel his pulse. What for? To save his life? Yes. In mercy? No; simply that they might rack him once again.

This was done, remember, in the name of civilization; in the name of law and order; in the name of mercy; in the name of religion; in the name of the most merciful Christ.

Sometimes, when I read and think about these

frightful things, it seems to me that I have suffered, all these horrors myself.   It seems sometimes, as though I had stood upon the shore of exile and gazed with tearful eyes toward home and native land; as though my nails had been torn from my hands, and into the bleeding quick needles had been thrust; as though my feet had been crushed in iron boots; as though I had been chained in the cell of the Inquisition and listened with dying ears for the coming footsteps of release; as though I had stood upon the scaffold and had seen the glittering axe fall upon me; as though I had been upon the rack and had seen, bending above me, the white faces of hypocrite priests; as though I had been taken from my fireside, from my wife and children, taken to the public square, chained; as though fagots had been piled about me; as though the flames had climbed around my limbs and scorched my eyes to blindness, and as though my ashes had been scattered to the four winds, by all the countless hands of hate.   And when I so feel, I swear that while I live I will do what little I can to preserve and to augment the liberties of man, woman, and child.

It is a question of justice, of mercy, of honesty,

of intellectual development. If there is a man in the world who is not willing to give to every human being every right he claims for himself, he is just so much nearer a barbarian than I am. It is a question of honesty. The man who is not willing to give to every other the same intellectual rights he claims for himself, is dishonest, selfish, and brutal.

It is a question of intellectual development. Whoever holds another man responsible for his honest thought, has a deformed and distorted brain. It is a question of intellectual development.

A little while ago I saw models of nearly everything that man has made. I saw models of all the water craft, from the rude dug-out in which floated a naked savage—one of our ancestors—a naked savage, with teeth two inches in length, with a spoonful of brains in the back of his head—I saw models of all the water craft of the world, from that dug-out up to a man-of-war, that carries a hundred guns and miles of canvas—from that dug-out to the steamship that turns its brave prow from the port of New York, with a compass like a conscience, crossing three thousand miles of billows without missing a throb or beat of its mighty iron heart.

I saw at the same time the weapons that man has made, from a club, such as was grasped by that same savage, when he crawled from his den in the ground and hunted a snake for his dinner; from that club to the boomerang, to the sword, to the cross-bow, to the blunderbuss, to the flint-lock, to the cap-lock, to the needle-gun, up to a cannon cast by Krupp, capable of hurling a ball weighing two thousand pounds through eighteen inches of solid steel.

I saw, too, the armor from the shell of a turtle, that one of our brave ancestors lashed upon his breast when he went to fight for his country; the skin of a porcupine, dried with the quills on, which this same savage pulled over his orthodox head, up to the shirts of mail, that were worn in the Middle Ages, that laughed at the edge of the sword and defied the point of the spear; up to a monitor clad in complete steel.

I saw at the same time, their musical instruments, from the tom-tom — that is, a hoop with a couple of strings of raw hide drawn across it — from that tom-tom, up to the instruments we have to-day, that make the common air blossom with melody.

I saw, too, their paintings, from a daub of yellow mud, to the great works which now adorn the galleries of the world. I saw also their sculpture, from the rude god with four legs, a half dozen arms, several noses, and two or three rows of ears, and one little, contemptible, brainless head, up to the figures of to-day—to the marbles that genius has clad in such a personality that it seems almost impudent to touch them without an introduction.

I saw their books—books written upon skins of wild beasts — upon shoulder-blades of sheep — books written upon leaves, upon bark, up to the splendid volumes that enrich the libraries of our day. When I speak of libraries, I think of the remark of Plato: "A house that has a library in it has a soul."

I saw their implements of agriculture, from a crooked stick that was attached to the horn of an ox by some twisted straw, to the agricultural implements of this generation, that make it possible for a man to cultivate the soil without being an ignoramus.

While looking upon these things I was forced to say that man advanced only as he mingled his thought with his labor,—only as he got into partnership with the forces of nature,—only as he learned to take advantage of his surroundings— only as he freed himself from the bondage of fear, —only as he depended upon himself—only as he lost confidence in the gods.

I saw at the same time a row of human skulls, from the lowest skull that has been found, the Neanderthal skull — skulls from Central Africa, skulls from the Bushmen of Australia — skulls from the farthest isles of the Pacific sea — up to the best skulls of the last generation;—and I noticed that there was the same difference between those skulls that there was between the *products* of those skulls, and I said to myself, "After all, it is a simple question of intellectual development." There was the same difference between those skulls, the lowest and highest skulls, that there was between the dug-out and the man-of-war and the steamship, between the club and the Krupp gun, between the yellow daub and the landscape, between the tom-tom and an opera by Verdi.

The first and lowest skull in this row was the den in which crawled the base and meaner instincts of mankind, and the last was a temple in which dwelt joy, liberty, and love.

It is all a question of brain, of intellectual development.

If we are nearer free than were our fathers, it is because we have better heads upon the average, and more brains in them.

Now, I ask you to be honest with me. It makes no difference to you what I believe, nor what I wish to prove. I simply ask you to be honest. Divest your minds, for a moment at least, of all religious prejudice. Act, for a few moments, as though you were men and women.

Suppose the king, if there was one, and the priest, if there was one, at the time this gentleman floated in the dug-out, and charmed his ears with the music of the tom-tom, had said: "That dug-out is the best boat that ever can be built by man; the pattern of that came from on high, from the great god of storm and flood, and any man who says that he can improve it by putting a mast in it, with a sail upon it, is an infidel, and shall be burned at the stake;" what, in your judgment—honor bright— would have been the effect upon the circumnavigation of the globe?

Suppose the king, if there was one, and the priest, if there was one—and I presume there was a priest, because it was a very ignorant age—suppose this king and priest had said: "That tom-tom is the most beautiful instrument of music of which any man can conceive; that is the kind of music they have in heaven; an angel sitting upon the edge of a fleecy cloud, golden in the setting sun, playing upon that tom-tom, became so enraptured, so entranced with her own music, that in a kind of ecstasy she dropped it—that is how we obtained it; and any man who says that it can be improved by putting a back and front to it, and four strings, and a bridge, and getting a bow of hair with rosin, is a blaspheming wretch, and shall die the death,"—I ask you, what effect would that have had upon music? If that course had been pursued, would the human ears, in your judgment, ever have been enriched with the divine symphonies of Beethoven?

Suppose the king, if there was one, and the priest, had said: "That crooked stick is the best plow that can be invented: the pattern of that plow was given to a pious farmer in a holy dream, and that twisted straw is the *ne plus ultra* of all twisted things, and any man who says he can make an improvement upon that plow, is an atheist;" what, in your judgment, would have been the effect upon the science of agriculture?

But the people said, and the king and priest said: "We want better weapons with which to kill our fellow-Christians; we want better plows, better music, better paintings, and whoever will give us better weapons, and better music, better houses to live in, better clothes, we will robe him in wealth, and crown him with honor." Every incentive was held out to every human being to improve these things. That is the reason the club has been changed to a cannon, the dug-out to a steamship, the daub to a painting; that is the reason that the piece of rough and broken stone finally became a glorified statue.

You must not, however, forget that the gentleman in the dug-out, the gentleman who was enraptured with the music of the tom-tom, and cultivated his land with a crooked stick, had a religion of his own. That gentlemen in the dug-out was orthodox. He was never troubled with doubts. He lived and died settled in his mind. He believed in hell; and he thought he would be far happier in heaven, if he could just lean over and see certain people who expressed doubts as to the truth of his creed, gently but everlastingly broiled and burned.

It is a very sad and unhappy fact that this man has had a great many intellectual descendants. It is also an unhappy fact in nature, that the ignorant multiply much faster than the intellectual. This fellow in the dug-out believed in a personal devil. His devil had a cloven hoof, a long tail, armed with a fiery dart; and his devil breathed brimstone. This devil was at least the equal of God; not quite so stout but a little shrewder. And do you know there has not been a patentable improvement made upon that devil for six thousand years.

This gentleman in the dug-out believed that God was a tyrant; that he would eternally damn the man who lived in accordance with his highest and grandest ideal. He believed that the earth was flat. He believed in a literal, burning, seething hell of fire and sulphur. He had also his idea of politics; and his doctrine was, might makes right. And it will take thousands of years before the world will reverse this doctrine, and believingly say, "Right makes might."

All I ask is the same privilege to improve upon that gentleman's theology as upon his musical instrument; the same right to improve upon his politics as upon his dug-out. That is all. I ask for the human soul the same liberty in every direction. That is the only crime I have committed. I say, let us think. Let each one express his thought. Let us become investigators, not followers, not cringers and crawlers. If there is in heaven an infinite being, he never will be satisfied with the worship of cowards and hypocrites. Honest unbelief, honest infidelity, honest atheism, will be a perfume in heaven when pious hypocrisy, no matter how religious it may be outwardly, will be a stench.

This is my doctrine: Give every other human being every right you claim for yourself. Keep your mind open to the influences of nature. Receive new thoughts with hospitality. Let us advance.

The religionist of to-day wants the ship of his soul to lie at the wharf of orthodoxy and rot in the sun. He delights to hear the sails of old opinions flap against the masts of old creeds. He loves to see the joints and the sides open and gape in the sun, and it is a kind of bliss for him to repeat again and again: "Do not disturb my opinions. Do not unsettle my mind; I have it all made up, and I want no infidelity. Let me go backward rather than forward."

As far as I am concerned I wish to be out on the high seas. I wish to take my chances with wind, and wave, and star. And I had rather go down in the glory and grandeur of the storm, than to rot in any orthodox harbor whatever.

After all, we are improving from age to age. The most orthodox people in this country two hundred years ago would have been burned for the crime of heresy. The ministers who denounce me for expressing my thought would have been in the Inquisition themselves. Where once burned and blazed the bivouac fires of the army of progress, now glow the altars of the church. The religionists of our time are occupying about the same ground occupied by heretics and infidels of one hundred years ago. The church has advanced in spite, as it were, of itself. It has followed the army of progress protesting and denouncing, and had to keep within protesting and denouncing distance. If the church had not made great progress I could not express my thoughts.

Man, however, has advanced just exactly in the proportion with which he has mingled his thought with his labor. The sailor, without control of the wind and wave, knowing nothing or very little of the mysterious currents and pulses of the sea, is superstitious. So also is the agriculturist, whose prosperity depends upon something he cannot control. But the mechanic, when a wheel refuses to turn, never thinks of dropping on his knees and asking the assistance of some divine power. He knows there is a reason. He knows that something is too large or too small; that there is something wrong with his machine; and he goes to work and he makes it larger or smaller, here or there, until the wheel will turn. Now, just in proportion as man gets away from being, as it were, the slave of his surroundings, the serf of the elements,—of the heat, the frost, the snow, and the lightning, — just to the extent that he has gotten control of his own destiny, just to the extent that he has triumphed over the obstacles of nature, he has advanced physically and intellectually. As man develops, he places a greater value upon his own rights. Liberty becomes a grander and diviner thing. As he values his own rights, he begins to value the rights of others. And when all men give to all others all the rights they claim for themselves, this world will be civilized.

A few years ago the people were afraid to

question the king, afraid to question the priest, afraid to investigate a creed, afraid to deny a book, afraid to denounce a dogma, afraid to reason, afraid to think. Before wealth they bowed to the very earth, and in the presence of titles they became abject. All this is slowly but surely changing. We no longer bow to men simply because they are rich. Our fathers worshiped the golden calf. The worst you can say of an American now is, he worships the gold of the calf. Even the calf is beginning to see this distinction.

It no longer satisfies the ambition of a great man to be king or emperor. The last Napoleon was not satisfied with being the emperor of the French. He was not satisfied with having a circlet of gold about his head. He wanted some evidence that he had something of value within his head. So he wrote the life of Julius Cæsar, that he might become a member of the French Academy. The emperors, the kings, the popes, no longer tower above their fellows. Compare King William with the philosopher Haeckel. The king is one of the anointed by the most high, as they claim—one upon whose head has been poured the divine petroleum of authority. Compare this king with

Haeckel, who towers an intellectual colossus above the crowned mediocrity. Compare George Eliot with Queen Victoria. The Queen is clothed in garments given her by blind fortune and unreasoning chance, while George Eliot wears robes of glory woven in the loom of her own genius.

The world is beginning to pay homage to intellect, to genius, to heart.

We have advanced. We have reaped the benefit of every sublime and heroic self-sacrifice, of every divine and brave act; and we should endeavor to hand the torch to the next generation, having added a little to the intensity and glory of the flame.

When I think of how much this world has suffered; when I think of how long our fathers were slaves, of how they cringed and crawled at the foot of the throne, and in the dust of the altar, of how they abased themselves, of how abjectly they stood in the presence of superstition robed and crowned, I am amazed.

This world has not been fit for a man to live in fifty years. It was not until the year 1808 that Great Britain abolished the slave trade. Up to that time her judges, sitting upon the bench in the

name of justice, her priests, occupying her pulpits,
in the name of universal love, owned stock in the
slave ships, and luxuriated upon the profits of
piracy and murder.   It was not until the same year
that the United States of America abolished the
slave trade between this and other countries, but
carefully preserved it as between the States.   It
was not until the 28th day of August, 1833, that
Great Britain abolished human slavery in her colo-
nies; and it was not until the 1st day of January,
1863, that Abraham Lincoln, sustained by the sublime and heroic North, rendered our flag pure as
the sky in which it floats.

Abraham Lincoln was, in my judgment, in many
respects, the grandest man ever President of the
United States.   Upon his monument these words
should be written: "Here sleeps the only man in
the history of the world, who, having been clothed
with almost absolute power, never abused it, except
upon the side of mercy."

Think how long we clung to the institution of
human slavery, how long lashes upon the naked
back were a legal tender for labor performed.
Think of it.   The pulpit of this country deliber-
ately and willingly, for a hundred years, turned the
cross of Christ into a whipping post.

With every drop of my blood I hate and execrate every form of tyranny, every form of slavery. I hate dictation. I love liberty.

What do I mean by liberty? By physical liberty I mean the right to do anything which does not interfere with the happiness of another. By intellectual liberty I mean the right to think right and the right to think wrong. Thought is the means by which we endeavor to arrive at truth. If we know the truth already, we need not think. All that can be required is honesty of purpose. You ask my opinion about anything; I examine it honestly, and when my mind is made up, what should I tell you? Should I tell you my real thought? What should I do? There is a book put in my hands. I am told this is the Koran; it was written by inspiration. I read it, and when I get through, suppose that I think in my heart and in my brain, that it is utterly untrue, and you then ask me, what do you think? Now, admitting that I live in Turkey, and have no chance to get any office unless I am on the side of the Koran, what should I say? Should I make a clean breast and say, that upon my honor I do not believe it? What would you think then of my fellow-citizens if they said: "That man is dangerous, he is dishonest."

Suppose I read the book called the Bible, and when I get through I make up my mind that it was written by men. A minister asks me, " Did you read the Bible? " I answer, that I did. " Do you think it divinely inspired? " What should I reply? Should I say to myself, " If I deny the inspiration of the Scriptures, the people will never clothe me with power." What ought I to answer? Ought I not to say like a man: "I have read it; I do not believe it." Should I not give the real transcript of my mind? Or should I turn hypocrite and pretend what I do not feel, and hate myself forever after for being a cringing coward. For my part I would rather a man would tell me what he honestly thinks. I would rather he would preserve his manhood. I had a thousand times rather be a manly unbeliever than an unmanly believer. And if there is a judgment day, a time when all will stand before some supreme being, I believe I will stand higher, and stand a better chance of getting my case decided in my favor, than any man sneaking through life pretending to believe what he does not.

I have made up my mind to say my say. I

shall do it kindly, distinctly; but I am going to do it. I know there are thousands of men who sub-stantially agree with me, but who are not in a con-dition to express their thoughts. They are poor; they are in business; and they know that should they tell their honest thought, persons will refuse to patronize them—to trade with them; they wish to get bread for their little children; they wish to take care of their wives; they wish to have homes and the comforts of life. Every such person is a certificate of the meanness of the community in which he resides. And yet I do not blame these people for not expressing their thought. I say to them: "Keep your ideas to yourselves; feed and clothe the ones you love; I will do your talking for you. The church can not touch, can not crush, can not starve, cannot stop or stay me; I will ex-press your thoughts."

As an excuse for tyranny, as a justification of slavery, the church has taught that man is totally depraved. Of the truth of that doctrine, the church has furnished the only evidence there is. The truth is, we are both good and bad. The worst are capable of some good deeds, and the

best are capable of bad. The lowest can rise, and
the highest may fall. That mankind can be divided
into two great classes, sinners and saints, is an
utter falsehood. In times of great disaster, called
it may be, by the despairing voices of women, men,
denounced by the church as totally depraved, rush
to death as to a festival. By such men, deeds
are done so filled with self-sacrifice and generous
daring, that millions pay to them the tribute, not
only of admiration, but of tears. Above all creeds,
above all religions, after all, is that divine thing,—
Humanity; and now and then in shipwreck on the
wide, wild sea, or 'mid the rocks and breakers of
some cruel shore, or where the serpents of flame
writhe and hiss, some glorious heart, some chivalric
soul does a deed that glitters like a star, and gives
the lie to all the dogmas of superstition. All these
frightful doctrines have been used to degrade and
to enslave mankind.

Away, forever away with the creeds and books
and forms and laws and religions that take from
the soul liberty and reason. Down with the idea
that thought is dangerous! Perish the infamous
doctrine that man can have property in man. Let
us resent with indignation every effort to put a

chain upon our minds. If there is no God, certainly we should not bow and cringe and crawl. If there is a God, there should be no slaves.

LIBERTY OF WOMAN.

Women have been the slaves of slaves; and in my judgment it took millions of ages for woman to come from the condition of abject slavery up to the institution of marriage. Let me say right here, that I regard marriage as the holiest institution among men. Without the fireside there is no human advancement; without the family relation there is no life worth living. Every good government is made up of good families. The unit of good government is the family, and anything that tends to destroy the family is perfectly devilish and infamous. I believe in marriage, and I hold in utter contempt the opinions of those long-haired men and short-haired women who denounce the institution of marriage.

The grandest ambition that any man can possibly have, is to so live, and so improve himself in heart and brain, as to be worthy of the love of some splendid woman; and the grandest ambition of any girl is to make herself worthy of the love and ado-

ration of some magnificent man.   That is my idea.
There is no success in life without love and marriage.   You had better be the emperor of one loving and tender heart, and she the empress of yours,
than to be king of the world.   The man who has
really won the love of one good woman in this
world, I do not care if he dies in the ditch a beggar, his life has been a success.

I say it took millions of years to come from the
condition of abject slavery up to the condition of
marriage.   Ladies, the ornaments you wear upon
your persons to-night are but the souvenirs of your
mother's bondage.   The chains around your necks,
and the bracelets clasped upon your white arms by
the thrilled hand of love, have been changed by
the wand of civilization from iron to shining, glittering gold.

But nearly every religion has accounted for all
the devilment in this world by the crime of woman.
What a gallant thing that is!   And if it is.true, I
had rather live with the woman I love in a world
full of trouble, than to live in heaven with nobody
but men.

I read in a book—and I will say now that I
cannot give the exact language, as my memory does

not retain the words, but I can give the substance —I read in a book that the Supreme Being concluded to make a world and one man; that he took some nothing and made a world and one man, and put this man in a garden. In a little while he noticed that the man got lonesome; that he wandered around as if he was waiting for a train. There was nothing to interest him; no news; no papers; no politics; no policy; and, as the devil had not yet made his appearance, there was no chance for reconciliation; not even for civil service reform. Well, he wandered about the garden in this condition, until finally the Supreme Being made up his mind to make him a companion.

Having used up all the nothing he originally took in making the world and one man, he had to take a part of the man to start a woman with. So he caused a sleep to fall on this man—now understand me, I do not say this story is true. After the sleep fell upon this man, the Supreme Being took a rib, or as the French would call it, a cutlet, out of this man, and from that he made a woman. And considering the amount of raw material used, I look upon it as the most successful job ever performed. Well, after he got the woman done, she was brought to the man; not to see how she liked him, but to see how he liked her. He liked her, and they started housekeeping; and they were told of certain things they might do and of one thing they could not do—and of course they did it. I would have done it in fifteen minutes, and I know it. There wouldn't have been an apple on that tree half an hour from date, and the limbs would have been full of clubs. And then they were turned out of the park and extra policemen were put on to keep them from getting back.

Devilment commenced. The mumps, and the measles, and the whooping-cough, and the scarlet fever started in their race for man. They began to have the toothache, roses began to have thorns, snakes began to have poisoned teeth, and people began to divide about religion and politics, and the world has been full of trouble from that day to this.

Nearly all of the religions of this world account for the existence of evil by such a story as that!

I read in another book what appeared to be an account of the same transaction. It was written about four thousand years before the other. All commentators agree that the one that was written last was the original, and that the one that was

written first was copied from the one that was
written last. But I would advise you all not to
allow your creed to be disturbed by a little matter
of four or five thousand years. In this other story,
Brahma made up his mind to make the world and a
man and woman. He made the world, and he
made the man and then the woman, and put them
on the island of Ceylon. According to the account
it was the most beautiful island of which man can
conceive. Such birds, such songs, such flowers and
such verdure! And the branches of the trees were
so arranged that when the wind swept through
them every tree was a thousand Æolian harps.

Brahma, when he put them there, said: "Let
them have a period of courtship, for it is my desire
and will that true love should forever precede
marriage." When I read that, it was so much
more beautiful and lofty than the other, that I said
to myself, "If either one of these stories ever turns
out to be true, I hope it will be this one."

Then they had their courtship, with the nightingale singing, and the stars shining, and the flowers
blooming, and they fell in love. Imagine that
courtship! No prospective fathers or mothers-in-
law; no prying and gossiping neighbors; nobody

to say, "Young man, how do you expect to support
her?" Nothing of that kind. They were married
by the Supreme Brahma, and he said to them:
"Remain here; you must never leave this island."
Well, after a little while the man—and his name
was Adami, and the woman's name was Heva—
said to Heva: "I believe I'll look about a little."
He went to the northern extremity of the island
where there was a little narrow neck of land con-
necting it with the mainland, and the devil, who is
always playing pranks with us, produced a mirage,
and when he looked over to the mainland, such
hills and vales, such dells and dales, such mountains
crowned with snow, such cataracts clad in bows of
glory did he see there, that he went back and told
Heva: "The country over there is a thousand
times better than this; let us migrate." She, like
every other woman that ever lived, said: "Let well
enough alone; we have all we want; let us stay
here." But he said "No, let us go;" so she followed him, and when they came to this narrow
neck of land, he took her on his back like a gentleman, and carried her over. But the moment
they got over they heard a crash, and looking back,
discovered that this narrow neck of land had fallen

into the sea. The mirage had disappeared, and there were naught but rocks and sand; and then the Supreme Brahma cursed them both to the lowest hell.

Then it was that the man spoke,—and I have liked him ever since for it—"Curse me, but curse not her, it was not her fault, it was mine."

That's the kind of man to start a world with.

The Supreme Brahma said: "I will save her, but not thee." And then she spoke out of her fullness of love, out of a heart in which there was love enough to make all her daughters rich in holy affection, and said: "If thou wilt not spare him, spare neither me; I do not wish to live without him; I love him." Then the Supreme Brahma said—and I have liked him ever since I read it—"I will spare you both and watch over you and your children forever."

Honor bright, is not that the better and grander story?

And from that same book I want to show you what ideas some of these miserable heathen had; the heathen we are trying to convert. We send missionaries over yonder to convert heathen there, and we send soldiers out on the plains to kill heathen here. If we can convert the heathen, why not convert those nearest home? Why not convert those we can get at? Why not convert those who have the immense advantage of the example of the average pioneer? But to show you the men we are trying to convert: In this book it says: " Man is strength, woman is beauty; man is courage, woman is love. When the one man loves the one woman and the one woman loves the one man, the very angels leave heaven and come and sit in that house and sing for joy."

They are the men we are converting. Think of it! I tell you, when I read these things, I say that love is not of any country; nobility does not belong exclusively to any race, and through all the ages, there have been a few great and tender souls blossoming in love and pity.

In my judgment, the woman is the equal of the man. She has all the rights I have and one more, and that is the right to be protected. That is my doctrine. You are married; try and make the woman you love happy. Whoever marries simply for himself will make a mistake; but whoever loves a woman so well that he says " I will make her happy," makes no mistake. And so with the woman who says, " I will make him happy." There is only one way to be happy, and that is to make somebody else so, and you cannot be happy by going cross lots ; you have got to go the regular turnpike road.

If there is any man I detest, it is the man who thinks he is the head of a family—the man who thinks he is " boss ! " The fellow in the dug-out used that word " boss ; " that was one of his favorite expressions.

Imagine a young man and a young woman courting, walking out in the moonlight, and the nightingale singing a song of pain and love, as though the thorn touched her heart—imagine them stopping there in the moonlight and starlight and song, and saying, " Now, here, let us settle who is ' boss ! ' " I tell you it is an infamous word and an infamous feeling—I abhor a man who is " boss," who is going to govern in his family, and when he speaks orders all the rest to be still as some mighty idea is about to be launched from his mouth. Do you know I dislike this man unspeakably ?

I hate above all things a cross man. What right has he to murder the sunshine of a day ? What right has he to assassinate the joy of life ?

When you go home you ought to go like a ray of light — so that it will, even in the night, burst out of the doors and windows and illuminate the darkness. Some men think their mighty brains have been in a turmoil; they have been thinking about who will be alderman from the fifth ward; they have been thinking about politics; great and mighty questions have been engaging their minds; they have bought calico at five cents or six, and want to sell it for seven. Think of the intellectual strain that must have been upon that man, and when he gets home everybody else in the house must look out for his comfort. A woman who has only taken care of five or six children, and one or two of them sick, has been nursing them and singing to them, and trying to make one yard of cloth do the work of two, she, of course, is fresh and fine and ready to wait upon this gentleman — the head of the family — the boss!

Do you know another thing? I despise a stingy man. I do not see how it is possible for a man to die worth fifty million of dollars, or ten million of dollars, in a city full of want, when he meets almost every day the withered hand of beggary and the white lips of famine. How a man can withstand all that, and hold in the clutch of his greed twenty or thirty million of dollars, is past my comprehension. I do not see how he can do it. I should not think he could do it any more than he could keep a pile of lumber on the beach, where hundreds and thousands of men were drowning in the sea.

Do you know that I have known men who would trust their wives with their hearts and their honor but not with their pocketbook; not with a dollar. When I see a man of that kind, I always think he knows which of these articles is the most valuable. Think of making your wife a beggar! Think of her having to ask you every day for a dollar, or for two dollars or fifty cents! "What did you do with that dollar I gave you last week?" Think of having a wife that is afraid of you! What kind of children do you expect to have with a beggar and a coward for their mother? Oh, I tell you if you have but a dollar in the world, and you have got to spend it, spend it like a king; spend it as though it were a dry leaf and you the owner of unbounded forests! That's the way to spend it! I had rather be a beggar and spend my last dollar like a king, than be a king and spend my money like a beggar! If it has got to go, let it go!

Get the best you can for your family—try to look as well as you can yourself. When you used to go courting, how elegantly you looked! Ah, your eye was bright, your step was light, and you looked like a prince. Do you know that it is insufferable egotism in you to suppose a woman is going to love you always looking as slovenly as you can! Think of it! Any good woman on earth will be true to you forever when you do your level best.

Some people tell me, " Your doctrine about loving, and wives, and all that, is splendid for the rich, but it won't do for the poor." I tell you to-night there is more love in the homes of the poor than in the palaces of the rich. The meanest hut with love in it is a palace fit for the gods, and a palace without love is a den only fit for wild beasts. That is my doctrine! You cannot be so poor that you cannot help somebody. Good nature is the cheapest commodity in the world; and love is the only thing that will pay ten per cent. to borrower and lender both. Do not tell me that you have got to be rich! We have a false standard of greatness in the United States. We think here that a man must be great, that he must be notorious; that he must be extremely wealthy, or that his name must be upon the putrid lips of rumor. It is all a mistake. It is not necessary to be rich or to be great, or to be powerful, to be happy. The happy man is the successful man.

Happiness is the legal tender of the soul.

Joy is wealth.

A little while ago, I stood by the grave of the old Napoleon — a magnificent tomb of gilt and gold, fit almost for a dead deity — and gazed upon the sarcophagus of rare and nameless marble, where rest at last the ashes of that restless man. I leaned over the balustrade and thought about the career of the greatest soldier of the modern world.

I saw him walking upon the banks of the Seine, contemplating suicide. I saw him at Toulon—I saw him putting down the mob in the streets of Paris—I saw him at the head of the army of Italy —I saw him crossing the bridge of Lodi with the tri-color in his hand—I saw him in Egypt in the shadows of the pyramids—I saw him conquer the Alps and mingle the eagles of France with the eagles of the crags. I saw him at Marengo—at

Ulm and Austerlitz. I saw him in Russia, where the infantry of the snow and the cavalry of the wild blast scattered his legions like winter's withered leaves. I saw him at Leipsic in defeat and disaster —driven by a million bayonets back upon Paris— clutched like a wild beast—banished to Elba. I saw him escape and retake an empire by the force of his genius. I saw him upon the frightful field of Waterloo, where Chance and Fate combined to wreck the fortunes of their former king. And I saw him at St. Helena, with his hands crossed behind him, gazing out upon the sad and solemn sea.

I thought of the orphans and widows he had made—of the tears that had been shed for his glory, and of the only woman who ever loved him, pushed from his heart by the cold hand of ambition. And I said I would rather have been a French peasant and worn wooden shoes. I would rather have lived in a hut with a vine growing over the door, and the grapes growing purple in the kisses of the autumn sun. I would rather have been that poor peasant with my loving wife by my side, knitting as the day died out of the sky—with my children upon my knees and their arms about me—I would rather have been that man and gone down to the tongueless silence of the dreamless dust, than to have been that imperial impersonation of force and murder, known as "Napoleon the Great."

It is not necessary to be great to be happy; it is not necessary to be rich to be just and generous and to have a heart filled with divine affection. No matter whether you are rich or poor, treat your wife as though she were a splendid flower, and she will fill your life with perfume and with joy.

And do you know, it is a splendid thing to think that the woman you really love will never grow old to you. Through the wrinkles of time, through the mask of years, if you really love her, you will always see the face you loved and won. And a woman who really loves a man does not see that he grows old; he is not decrepit to her; he does not tremble; he is not old; she always sees the same gallant gentleman who won her hand and heart. I like to think of it in that way; I like to think that love is eternal. And to love in that way and then go down the hill of life together, and as you go down, hear, perhaps, the laughter of grandchildren, while the birds of joy and love sing once more in the leafless branches of the tree of age.

I believe in the fireside. I believe in the democracy of home. I believe in the republicanism of the family. I believe in liberty, equality and love.

THE LIBERTY OF CHILDREN.

If women have been slaves, what shall I say of children; of the little children in alleys and sub-cellars; the little children who turn pale when they hear their fathers' footsteps; little children who run away when they only hear their names called by the lips of a mother; little children—the children of poverty, the children of crime, the children of brutality, wherever they are—flotsam and jetsam upon the wild, mad sea of life—my heart goes out to them, one and all.

I tell you the children have the same rights that we have, and we ought to treat them as though they were human beings. They should be reared with love, with kindness, with tenderness, and not with brutality. That is my idea of children.

When your little child tells a lie, do not rush at him as though the world were about to go into bankruptcy. Be honest with him. A tyrant father will have liars for his children; do you know that?

A lie is born of tyranny upon the one hand and weakness upon the other, and when you rush at a poor little boy with a club in your hand, of course he lies.

I thank thee, Mother Nature, that thou hast put ingenuity enough in the brain of a child, when attacked by a brutal parent, to throw up a little breastwork in the shape of a lie.

When one of your children tells a lie, be honest with him; tell him that you have told hundreds of them yourself. Tell him it is not the best way; that you have tried it. Tell him as the man did in Maine when his boy left home: "John, honesty is the best policy; I have tried both." Be honest with him. Suppose a man as much larger than you as you are larger than a child five years old, should come at you with a liberty pole in his hand, and in a voice of thunder shout, "Who broke that plate?" There is not a solitary one of you who would not swear you never saw it, or that it was cracked when you got it. Why not be honest with these children? Just imagine a man who deals in stocks whipping his boy for putting false rumors afloat! Think of a lawyer beating his own flesh and blood for evading the truth when he makes half of his own living that way! Think of a minister punishing his child for not telling all he thinks! Just think of it!

When your child commits a wrong, take it in your arms; let it feel your heart beat against its heart; let the child know that you really and truly and sincerely love it. Yet some Christians, good Christians, when a child commits a fault, drive it from the door and say: "Never do you darken this house again." Think of that! And then these same people will get down on their knees and ask God to take care of the child they have driven from home. I will never ask God to take care of my children unless I am doing my level best in that same direction.

But I will tell you what I say to my children: "Go where you will; commit what crime you may; fall to what depth of degradation you may; you can never commit any crime that will shut my door, my arms, or my heart to you. As long as I live you shall have one sincere friend."

Do you know that I have seen some people who acted as though they thought that when the Savior said "Suffer little children to come unto me, for of such is the kingdom of heaven," he had a raw-hide under his mantle, and made that remark simply to get the children within striking distance?

I do not believe in the government of the lash. If any one of you ever expects to whip your children again, I want you to have a photograph taken of yourself when you are in the act, with your face red with vulgar anger, and the face of the little child, with eyes swimming in tears and the little chin dimpled with fear, like a piece of water struck by a sudden cold wind. Have the picture taken. If that little child should die, I cannot think of a sweeter way to spend an autumn afternoon than to go out to the cemetery, when the maples are clad in tender gold, and little scarlet runners are coming, like poems of regret, from the sad heart of the earth—and sit down upon the grave and look at that photograph, and think of the flesh now dust that you beat. I tell you it is wrong; it is no way to raise children! Make your home happy. Be honest with them. Divide fairly with them in everything.

Give them a little liberty and love, and you can not drive them out of your house. They will want to stay there. Make home pleasant. Let them play any game they wish. Do not be so foolish as to say : " You may roll balls on the ground, but you must not roll them on a green cloth. You may knock them with a mallet, but you must not push them with a cue. You may play with little pieces of paper which have ' authors ' written on them, but you must not have ' cards.' " Think of it! " You may go to a minstrel show where people blacken themselves and imitate humanity below them, but you must not go to a theatre and see the characters created by immortal genius put upon the stage." Why? Well, I can't think of any reason in the world except " minstrel " is a word of two syllables, and " theatre " has three.

Let children have some daylight at home if you want to keep them there, and do not commence at the cradle and shout " Don't! " " Don't! " " Stop! " That is nearly all that is said to a child from the cradle until he is twenty-one years old, and when he comes of age other people begin saying " Don't! " And the church says " Don't! " and the party he belongs to says " Don't! "

I despise that way of going through this world. Let us have liberty—just a little. Call me infidel, call me atheist, call me what you will, I intend so to treat my children, that they can come to my grave and truthfully say: " He who sleeps here never gave us a moment of pain. From his lips, now dust, never came to us an unkind word."

People justify all kinds of tyranny toward children upon the ground that they are totally depraved. At the bottom of ages of cruelty lies this infamous doctrine of total depravity. Religion contemplates a child as a living crime—heir to an infinite curse—doomed to eternal fire.

In the olden time, they thought some days were too good for a child to enjoy himself. When I was a boy Sunday was considered altogether too holy to be happy in. Sunday used to commence then when the sun went down on Saturday night. We commenced at that time for the purpose of getting a good ready, and when the sun fell below the horizon on Saturday evening, there was a darkness fell upon the house ten thousand times deeper than that of night. Nobody said a pleasant word; nobody laughed; nobody smiled; the child that looked the sickest was regarded as the most pious. That night you could not even crack hickory nuts. If you were caught chewing gum it was only another evidence of the total depravity of the human heart. It was an exceedingly solemn night.

Dyspepsia was in the very air you breathed. Everybody looked sad and mournful. I have noticed all my life that many people think they have religion when they are troubled with dyspepsia. If there could be found an absolute specific for that disease, it would be the hardest blow the church has ever received.

On Sunday morning the solemnity had simply increased. Then we went to church. The minister was in a pulpit about twenty feet high, with a little sounding-board above him, and he commenced at "firstly" and went on and on and on to about "twenty-thirdly." Then he made a few remarks by way of application; and then took a general view of the subject, and in about two hours reached the last chapter in Revelation.

In those days, no matter how cold the weather was, there was no fire in the church. It was thought to be a kind of sin to be comfortable while you were thanking God. The first church that ever had a stove in it in New England, divided on that account. So the first church in which they sang by note, was torn in fragments.

After the sermon we had an intermission. Then came the catechism with the chief end of

nan. We went through with that. We sat in a
row with our feet coming in about six inches of the
door. The minister asked us if we knew that we
all deserved to go to hell, and we all answered
'Yes." Then we were asked if we would be will-
ng to go to hell if it was God's will, and every little
iar shouted " Yes." Then the same sermon was
preached once more, commencing at the other end
and going back. After that, we started for home,
sad and solemn—overpowered with the wisdom
displayed in the scheme of the atonement. When
we got home, if we had been good boys, and the
weather was warm, sometimes they would take us
out to the graveyard to cheer us up a little. It did
cheer me. When I looked at the sunken tombs
and the leaning stones, and read the half-effaced
inscriptions through the moss of silence and forget-
fulness, it was a great comfort. The reflection
came to my mind that the observance of the Sab-
bath could not last always. Sometimes they would
sing that beautiful hymn in which occurs these
cheerful lines:

> "Where congregations ne'er break up,
> And Sabbaths never end."

These lines, I think, prejudiced me a little

against even heaven. Then we had good books that we read on Sundays by way of keeping us happy and contented. There were Milners' "History of the Waldenses," Baxter's "Call to the Unconverted," Yahn's "Archæology of the Jews," and Jenkyns' "On the Atonement." I used to read Jenkyns' "On the Atonement." I have often thought that an atonement would have to be exceedingly broad in its provisions to cover the case of a man who would write a book like that for a boy.

But at last the Sunday wore away, and the moment the sun went down we were free. Between three and four o'clock we would go out to see how the sun was coming on. Sometimes it seemed to me that it was stopping from pure meanness. But finally it went down. It had to. And when the last rim of light sank below the horizon, off would go our caps, and we would give three cheers for liberty once more.

Sabbaths used to be prisons. Every Sunday was a Bastile. Every Christian was a kind of turn-key, and every child was a prisoner,—a convict. In that dungeon, a smile was a crime.

It was thought wrong for a child to laugh upon this holy day. Think of that!

A little child would go out into the garden, and there would be a tree laden with blossoms, and the little fellow would lean against it, and there would be a bird on one of the boughs, singing and swinging, and thinking about four little speckled eggs, warmed by the breast of its mate,—singing and swinging, and the music in happy waves rippling out of its tiny throat, and the flowers blossoming, the air filled with perfume and the great white clouds floating in the sky, and the little boy would lean up against that tree and think about hell and the worm that never dies.

I have heard them preach, when I sat in the pew and my feet did not touch the floor, about the final home of the unconverted. In order to impress upon the children the length of time they would probably stay if they settled in that country, the preacher would frequently give us the following illustration: "Suppose that once in a billion years a bird should come from some far-distant planet, and carry off in its little bill a grain of sand, a time would finally come when the last atom composing this earth would be carried away; and when this

last atom was taken, it would not even be sun
up in hell." Think of such an infamous doctrine
being taught to children!

The laugh of a child will make the holiest day
more sacred still. Strike with 'hand of fire, O
weird musician, thy harp strung with Apollo's
golden hair; fill the vast cathedral aisles with
symphonies sweet and dim, deft toucher of the
organ keys; blow, bugler, blow, until thy silver
notes do touch and kiss the moonlit waves, and
charm the lovers wandering 'mid the vine-clad hills.
But know, your sweetest strains are discords all,
compared with childhood's happy laugh—the laugh
that fills the eyes with light and every heart with
joy. O rippling river of laughter, thou art the
blessed boundary line between the beasts and men;
and every wayward wave of thine doth drown some
fretful fiend of care. O Laughter, rose-lipped
daughter of Joy, there are dimples enough in thy
cheeks to catch and hold and glorify all the tears
of grief.

And yet the minds of children have been
polluted by this infamous doctrine of eternal
punishment. I denounce it to-day as a doctrine,
the infamy of which no language is sufficient to
express.

Where did that doctrine of eternal punishment for men and women and children come from? It came from the low and beastly skull of that wretch in the dug-out. Where did he get it? It was a souvenir from the animals. The doctrine of eternal punishment was born in the glittering eyes of snakes—snakes that hung in fearful coils watching for their prey. It was born of the howl and bark and growl of wild beasts. It was born of the grin of hyenas and of the depraved chatter of unclean baboons. I despise it with every drop of my blood. Tell me there is a God in the serene heavens that will damn his children for the expression of an honest belief! More men have died in their sins, judged by your orthodox creeds, than there are leaves on all the forests in the wide world ten thousand times over. Tell me these men are in hell; that these men are in torment; that these children are in eternal pain, and that they are to be punished forever and forever! I denounce this doctrine as the most infamous of lies.

When the great ship containing the hopes and aspirations of the world, when the great ship freighted with mankind goes down in the night of death, chaos and disaster, I am willing to go down with the ship. I will not be guilty of the ineffable meanness of paddling away in some orthodox canoe. I will go down with the ship, with those who love me, and with those whom I have loved. If there is a God who will damn his children forever, I would rather go to hell than to go to heaven and keep the society of such an infamous tyrant. I make my choice now. I despise that doctrine. It has covered the cheeks of this world with tears. It has polluted the hearts of children, and poisoned the imaginations of men. It has been a constant pain, a perpetual terror to every good man and woman and child. It has filled the good with horror and with fear; but it has had no effect upon the infamous and base. It has wrung the hearts of the tender ; it has furrowed the cheeks of the good. This doctrine never should be preached again. What right have you, sir, Mr. clergyman, you, minister of the gospel, to stand at the portals of the tomb, at the vestibule of eternity, and fill the future with horror and with fear? I do not believe this doctrine: neither do you. If you did, you could not sleep one moment. Any man who believes it, and has within his breast a decent, throbbing heart, will go insane. A man who believes that doctrine and does not go insane has the heart of a snake and the conscience of a hyena.

Jonathan Edwards, the dear old soul, who, if his doctrine is true, is now in heaven rubbing his holy hands with glee, as he hears the cries of the damned, preached this doctrine; and he said: "Can the believing husband in heaven be happy with his unbelieving wife in hell? Can the believing father in heaven be happy with his unbelieving children in hell? Can the loving wife in heaven be happy with her unbelieving husband in hell?" And he replies: "I tell you, yea. Such will be their sense of justice, that it will increase rather than diminish their bliss." There is no wild beast in the jungles of Africa whose reputation would not be tarnished by the expression of such a doctrine.

These doctrines have been taught in the name of religion, in the name of universal forgiveness, in the name of infinite love and charity. Do not, I pray you, soil the minds of your children with this dogma. Let them read for themselves; let them think for themselves.

Do not treat your children like orthodox posts

to be set in a row. Treat them like trees that need light and sun and air. Be fair and honest with them; give them a chance. Recollect that their rights are equal to yours. Do not have it in your mind that you must govern them; that they must obey. Throw away forever the idea of master and slave.

In old times they used to make the children go to bed when they were not sleepy, and get up when they were sleepy. I say let them go to bed when they are sleepy, and get up when they are not sleepy.

But you say, this doctrine will do for the rich but not for the poor. Well, if the poor have to waken their children early in the morning it is as easy to wake them with a kiss as with a blow. Give your children freedom; let them preserve their individuality. Let your children eat what they desire, and commence at the end of a dinner they like. That is their business and not yours. They know what they wish to eat. If they are given their liberty from the first, they know what they want better than any doctor in the world can prescribe. Do you know that all the improvement that has ever been made in the practice of medicine has been made by the recklessness of patients and not by the doctors? For thousands and thousands of years the doctors would not let a man suffering from fever have a drop of water. Water they looked upon as poison. But every now and then some man got reckless and said, "I had rather die than not to slake my thirst." Then he would drink two or three quarts of water and get well. And when the doctor was told of what the patient had done, he expressed great surprise that he was still alive, and complimented his constitution upon being able to bear such a frightful strain. The reckless men, however, kept on drinking the water, and persisted in getting well. And finally the doctors said: "In a fever, water is the very best thing you can take." So, I have more confidence in the voice of nature about such things than I have in the conclusions of the medical schools.

Let your children have freedom and they will fall into your ways; they will do substantially as you do; but if you try to make them, there is some magnificent, splendid thing in the human heart that refuses to be driven. And do you know that it is the luckiest thing that ever happened for this world, that people are that way. What would have become of the people five hundred years ago if they had followed strictly the advice of the doctors? They would have all been dead. What would the people have been, if at any age of the world they had followed implicitly the direction of the church? They would have all been idiots. It is a splendid thing that there is always some grand man who will not mind, and who will think for himself.

I believe in allowing the children to think for themselves. I believe in the democracy of the family. If in this world there is anything splendid, it is a home where all are equals.

You will remember that only a few years ago parents would tell their children to "let their victuals stop their mouths." They used to eat as though it were a religious ceremony — a very solemn thing. Life should not be treated as a solemn matter. I like to see the children at table, and hear each one telling of the wonderful things he has seen and heard. I like to hear the clatter of knives and forks and spoons mingling with their happy voices. I had rather hear it than any opera that was ever put upon the boards. Let the children have liberty. Be honest and fair with them; be just; be tender, and they will make you rich in love and joy.

Men are oaks, women are vines, children are flowers.

The human race has been guilty of almost countless crimes; but I have some excuse for mankind. This world, after all, is not very well adapted to raising good people. In the first place, nearly all of it is water. It is much better adapted to fish culture than to the production of folks. Of that portion which is land not one-eighth has suitable soil and climate to produce great men and women. You cannot raise men and women of genius, without the proper soil and climate, any more than you can raise corn and wheat upon the ice fields of the Arctic sea. You must have the necessary conditions and surroundings. Man is a product; you must have the soil and food. The obstacles presented by nature must not be so great that man cannot, by reasonable industry and courage, overcome them. There is upon this world only a narrow belt of land, circling zigzag the globe, upon which you can produce men and women of talent. In the Southern Hemisphere

the real climate that man needs falls mostly upon
the sea, and the result is, that the southern half of
our world has never produced a man or woman of
great genius.   In the far north there is no genius
—it is too cold.   In the far south there is no
genius—it is too warm.   There must be winter,
and there must be summer.   In a country where
man needs no coverlet but a cloud, revolution is
his normal condition.   Winter is the mother of
industry and prudence.   Above all, it is the mother
of the family relation.   Winter holds in its icy arms
the husband and wife and the sweet children.   If
upon this earth we ever have a glimpse of heaven,
it is when we pass a home in winter, at night, and
through the windows, the curtains drawn aside, we
see the family about the pleasant hearth; the old
lady knitting; the cat playing with the yarn; the
children wishing they had as many dolls or dollars
or knives or somethings, as there are sparks going
out to join the roaring blast; the father reading
and smoking, and the clouds rising like incense
from the altar of domestic joy.   I never passed
such a house without feeling that I had received a
benediction.

Civilization, liberty, justice, charity, intellectual

advancement, are all flowers that blossom in the drifted snow.

I do not know that I can better illustrate the great truth that only part of the world is adapted to the production of great men and women than by calling your attention to the difference between vegetation in valleys and upon mountains. In the valley you find the oak and elm tossing their branches defiantly to the storm, and as you advance up the mountain side the hemlock, the pine, the birch, the spruce, the fir, and finally you come to little dwarfed trees, that look like other trees seen through a telescope reversed — every limb twisted as though in pain — getting a scanty subsistence from the miserly crevices of the rocks. You go on and on, until at last the highest crag is freckled with a kind of moss, and vegetation ends. You might as well try to raise oaks and elms where the mosses grow, as to raise great men and great women where their surroundings are unfavorable. You must have the proper climate and soil.

A few years ago we were talking about the annexation of Santo Domingo to this country. I was in Washington at the time. I was opposed to it. I was told that it was a most delicious climate;

that the soil produced everything.   But I said:
"We do not want it; it is not the right kind of
country in which to raise American citizens.   Such
a climate would debauch us.   You might go there
with five thousand Congregational preachers, five
thousand ruling elders, five thousand professors in
colleges, five thousand of the solid men of Boston
and their wives; settle them all in Santo Domingo,
and you will see the second generation riding upon
a mule, bareback, no shoes, a grapevine bridle, hair
sticking out at the top of their sombreros, with a
rooster under each arm, going to a cock fight on
Sunday."   Such is the influence of climate.

Science, however, is gradually widening the
area within which men of genius can be produced.
We are conquering the north with houses, clothing,
food and fuel.   We are in many ways overcoming
the heat of the south.   If we attend to this world
instead of another, we may in time cover the land
with men and women of genius.

I have still another excuse.   I believe that man
came up from the lower animals.   I do not say this
as a fact.   I simply say I believe it to be a fact.
Upon that question I stand about eight to seven,
which, for all practical purposes, is very near a

certainty. When I first heard of that doctrine I did not like it. My heart was filled with sympathy for those people who have nothing to be proud of except ancestors. I thought, how terrible this will be upon the nobility of the Old World. Think of their being forced to trace their ancestry back to the duke Orang Outang, or to the princess Chimpanzee. After thinking it all over, I came to the conclusion that I liked that doctrine. I became convinced in spite of myself. I read about rudimentary bones and muscles. I was told that everybody had rudimentary muscles extending from the ear into the cheek. I asked " What are they?" I was told: "They are the remains of muscles; that they became rudimentary from lack of use; they went into bankruptcy. They are the muscles with which your ancestors used to flap their ears." I do not now so much wonder that we once had them as that we have outgrown them.

After all I had rather belong to a race that started from the skull-less vertebrates in the dim Laurentian seas, vertebrates wiggling without knowing why they wiggled, swimming without knowing where they were going, but that in some way began to develop, and began to get a little

higher and a little higher in the scale of existence;
that came up by degrees through millions of ages
through all the animal world, through all that crawls
and swims and floats and climbs and walks, and
finally produced the gentleman in the dug-out ; and
then from this man, getting a little grander, and
each one below calling every one above him a
heretic, calling every one who had made a little
advance an infidel or an atheist—for in the history
of this world the man who is ahead has always
been called a heretic—I would rather come from a
race that started from that skull-less vertebrate, and
came up and up and up and finally produced
Shakespeare, the man who found the human intellect dwelling in a hut, touched it with the wand of
his genius and it became a palace domed and
pinnacled; Shakespeare, who harvested all the
fields of dramatic thought, and from whose day to
this, there have been only gleaners of straw and
chaff—I would rather belong to that race that
commenced a skull-less vertebrate and produced
Shakespeare, a race that has before it an infinite
future, with the angel of progress leaning from the
far horizon, beckoning men forward, upward and
onward forever—I had rather belong to such a

race, commencing there, producing this, and with that hope, than to have sprung from a perfect pair upon which the Lord has lost money every moment from that day to this.

CONCLUSION.

I have given you my honest thought. Surely investigation is better than unthinking faith. Surely reason is a better guide than fear. This world should be controlled by the living, not by the dead. The grave is not a throne, and a corpse is not a king. Man should not try to live on ashes.

The theologians dead, knew no more than the theologians now living. More than this cannot be said. About this world little is known,— about another world, nothing.

Our fathers were intellectual serfs, and their fathers were slaves. The makers of our creeds were ignorant and brutal. Every dogma that we have, has upon it the mark of whip, the rust of chain, and the ashes of fagot.

Our fathers reasoned with instruments of torture. They believed in the logic of fire and sword. They hated reason. They despised thought. They abhorred liberty.

Superstition is the child of slavery. Free thought will give us truth. When all have the right to think and to express their thoughts, every brain will give to all the best it has. The world will then be filled with intellectual wealth.

As long as men and women are afraid of the church, as long as a minister inspires fear, as long as people reverence a thing simply because they do not understand it, as long as it is respectable to lose your self-respect, as long as the church has power, as long as mankind worship a book, just so long will the world be filled with intellectual paupers and vagrants, covered with the soiled and faded rags of superstition.

As long as woman regards the Bible as the charter of her rights, she will be the slave of man. The Bible was not written by a woman. Within its lids there is nothing but humiliation and shame for her. She is regarded as the property of man. She is made to ask forgiveness for becoming a mother. She is as much below her husband, as her husband is below Christ. She is not allowed to speak. The gospel is too pure to be spoken by her polluted lips. Woman should learn in silence.

In the Bible will be found no description of a

civilized home. The free mother surrounded by free and loving children, adored by a free man, her husband, was unknown to the inspired writers of the Bible. They did not believe in the democracy of home—in the republicanism of the fireside.

These inspired gentlemen knew nothing of the rights of children. They were the advocates of brute force—the disciples of the lash. They knew nothing of human rights. Their doctrines have brutalized the homes of millions, and filled the eyes of infancy with tears.

Let us free ourselves from the tyranny of a book, from the slavery of dead ignorance, from the aristocracy of the air.

There has never been upon the earth a generation of free men and women. It is not yet time to write a creed. Wait until the chains are broken —until dungeons are not regarded as temples. Wait until solemnity is not mistaken for wisdom— until mental cowardice ceases to be known as reverence. Wait until the living are considered the equals of the dead—until the cradle takes precedence of the coffin. Wait until what we know can be spoken without regard to what others may believe. Wait until teachers take the place of preachers — until followers become investigators. Wait until the world is free before you write a creed.

In this creed there will be but one word — Liberty.

Oh Liberty, float not forever in the far horizon — remain not forever in the dream of the enthusiast, the philanthropist and poet, but come and make thy home among the children of men!

I know not what discoveries, what inventions, what thoughts may leap from the brain of the world. I know not what garments of glory may be woven by the years to come. I cannot dream of the victories to be won upon the fields of thought; but I do know, that coming from the infinite sea of the future, there will never touch this "bank and shoal of time" a richer gift, a rarer blessing than liberty for man, for woman, and for child.

A TRIBUTE

TO

EBON C. INGERSOLL,

BY HIS BROTHER

ROBERT.

Dec. 12, 1831.   MAY 31, 1879.

A Tribute to Ebon C. Ingersoll,

By his Brother Robert.

THE RECORD OF A GENEROUS LIFE RUNS LIKE A VINE AROUND THE MEMORY OF OUR DEAD, AND EVERY SWEET, UNSELFISH ACT IS NOW A PERFUMED FLOWER.

DEAR FRIENDS : I am going to do that which the dead oft promised he would do for me.

The loved and loving brother, husband, father, friend, died where manhood's morning almost touches noon, and while the shadows still were falling toward the west.

He had not passed on life's highway the stone that marks the highest point ; but, being weary for a moment, he lay down by the wayside, and, using his burden for a pillow, fell into that dreamless sleep that kisses down his eyelids still. While yet in love with life and raptured with the world, he passed to silence and pathetic dust.

Yet, after all, it may be best, just in the happiest, sunniest hour of all the voyage, while eager winds are kissing every sail, to dash against the unseen rock, and in an instant hear the billows roar above a sunken ship. For whether in mid sea or 'mong the breakers of the farther shore, a wreck at last must mark the end of each and all. And every life, no matter if its every hour is rich with love and every moment jeweled with a joy, will, at its close, become a tragedy as sad and deep and dark as can be woven of the warp and woof of mystery and death.

This brave and tender man in every storm of life was oak and rock; but in the sunshine he was vine and flower. He was the friend of all heroic souls. He climbed the heights, and left all superstitions far below, while on his forehead fell the golden dawning of the grander day.

He loved the beautiful, and was with color, form, and music touched to tears. He sided with the weak, the poor, and wronged, and lovingly gave alms. With loyal heart and with the purest hands he faithfully discharged all public trusts.

He was a worshipper of liberty, a friend of the oppressed. A thousand times I have heard him quote these words : "*For Justice all place a temple, and all season, summer.*" He believed that happiness was the only good, reason the only torch, justice the only worship, humanity the only religion, and love the only priest. He added to the sum of human joy; and were every one to whom he did some loving service to bring a blossom to his grave, he would sleep to-night beneath a wilderness of flowers.

Life is a narrow vale between the cold and barren peaks of two eternities. We strive in vain to look beyond the heights. We cry aloud, and the only answer is the echo of our wailing cry. From the voiceless lips of the unreplying dead there comes no word ; but in the night of death hope sees a star and listening love can hear the rustle of a wing.

He who sleeps here, when dying, mistaking the approach of death for the return of health, whispered

with his latest breath, " I am better now." Let us
believe, in spite of doubts and dogmas, of fears and
tears, that these dear words are true of all the countless dead.

And now, to you, who have been chosen, from
among the many men he loved, to do the last sad
office for the dead, we give his sacred dust.

Speech cannot contain our love. There was
there is, no gentler, stronger, manlier man.

Just Published

ONLY AUTHORIZED EDITION

In one volume, large octavo, large type,
582 pages, price $2.50 net, postage 25c.

All of Colonel Ingersoll's Political Speeches contained in Volume IX of the Dresden Edition

* *"When the sword is drawn, reason remains in the scabbard."*

CONTENTS

*Page 259.   OVER

Address to the 86th Illinois Regiment—1865.

Decoration Day Address, New York City—1882.

Decoration Day Oration, New York City—1888.

Ratification Speech, Harrison and Morton Campaign—1888.

Reunion Address to the 11th Illinois Cavalry, of which Colonel Ingersoll was the Commanding Officer—1895.

The Chicago and New York Gold Speech—1896.

The voluminous and illuminating foot notes descriptive of the occasions upon which the different addresses were delivered are exceedingly valuable, bringing, as they do, those occasions vividly to the mind of the reader.

"Colonel Ingersoll writes with a rare and enviable brilliancy."
WM. E. GLADSTONE.

"Ingersoll was not only America's greatest orator. He was a great writer and a great thinker. His style is vigorous, as clear as it is graceful, as poetic as it is humorous, and as verve as inexhaustible."
MAX O'RELL.

"Of orators of the first class we have not had many. Ingersoll was one of them. Perhaps he was our supreme orator. In humor, persuasiveness, grace, power, majesty, he was the equal of the best."
ORLANDO J. SMITH, President American Press Association.

"I take the liberty of saying that I respect Ingersoll as the man who for a full score and more of years has worked for the right in the great, broad field of humanity, and for the sake of human rights, . . . The man who—and I say it not flatteringly—is the most brilliant speaker of the English tongue of all men on this globe. But as under the brilliancy of the blaze of light we find the living coals of fire, under the lambent flow of his wit and magnificent antithesis we find the glorious flame of genius and honest thought."
HENRY WARD BEECHER.

"Robert Ingersoll's was a great and beautiful spirit; he was a man—all man, from his crown to his foot soles. My reverence for him was deep and genuine. I prized his affection for me, and returned it with usury."
MARK TWAIN.

C. P. FARRELL

117 East 21st Street, New York City, N. Y.

Just Out.   Eighth E

Prose--Poems and Selections,

By ROBERT G. INGERSOLL

Revised and greatly Enlarged.   A Handsome 8vo. containing 427 pages.

THIS is, beyond question, the most elegant volume in Liberal literature. No expense has been spared to make it the thing of beauty that it is. The type is large and clear, the paper genuine water-marked Spartan, all-rag featherweight, pure white, deckle-edge, the presswork is faultless, and the binding as perfect as the best materials and skill can make it. The book is in every way an artistic triumph.

As to the contents, it is enough to say that they include some of the very choicest utterances of the greatest writer on the topics treated that has ever lived.

You will have in this book of selections many bright samples of his lofty thought, his matchless eloquence, his wonderful imagery, and his epigrammatic and poetic power.

The book is designed for, and will be accepted by admiring friends as a rare individual souvenir. To help it serve this purpose, a fine steel portrait, with autograph fac-simile, has been prepared especially for it. In the more elegant styles of binding it is eminently suited for presentation purposes, for any season or occasion.

CONTENTS

4

CPSIA information can be obtained
at www.ICGtesting.com
Printed in the USA
BVHW061655191222
654560BV00003B/75